THE PIANO GUYS
A Family Christmas

Visit The Piano Guys at:
the pianoguys.com

ISBN 978-1-4803-6233-8

HAL•LEONARD®
CORPORATION
7777 W. BLUEMOUND RD. P.O. BOX 13819 MILWAUKEE, WI 53213

In Australia Contact:
Hal Leonard Australia Pty. Ltd.
4 Lentara Court
Cheltenham, Victoria, 3192 Australia
Email: ausadmin@halleonard.com.au

Visit Hal Leonard Online at
www.halleonard.com

As performed by The Piano Guys

ANGELS WE HAVE HEARD ON HIGH

Arranged by JON SCH...
AL VAN DER BEEK and STEVEN SHARP N...

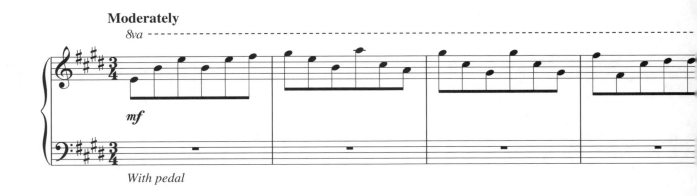

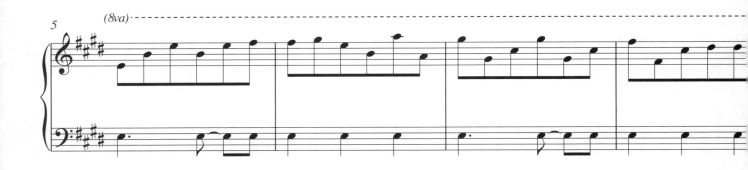

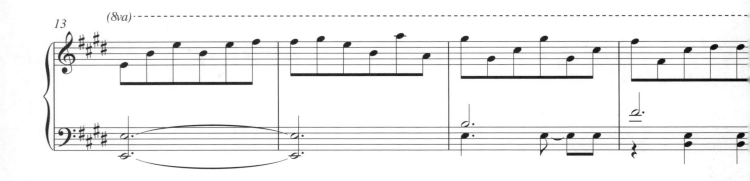

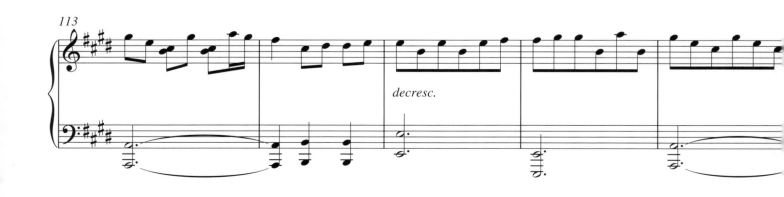

As performed by The Piano Guys

O COME O COME EMMANUEL

Arranged by MARSHALL McDONALD
and STEVEN SHARP NELSON
Adapted by JON SCHMIDT

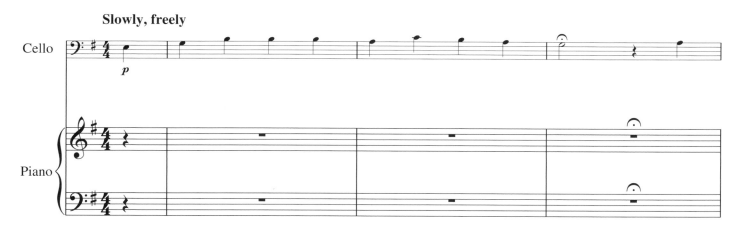

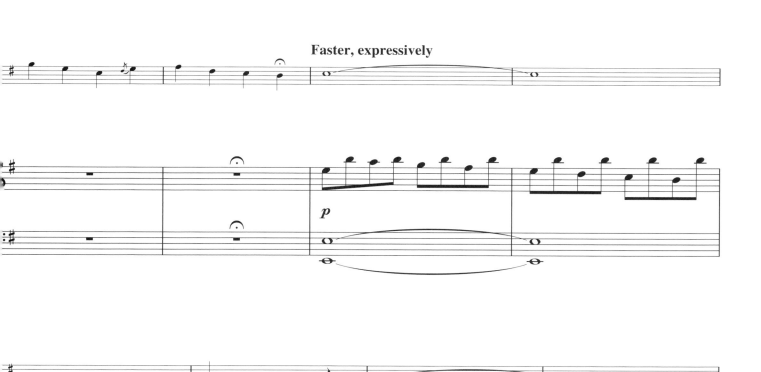

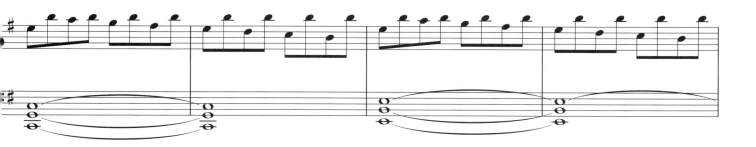

Slower

Moderately

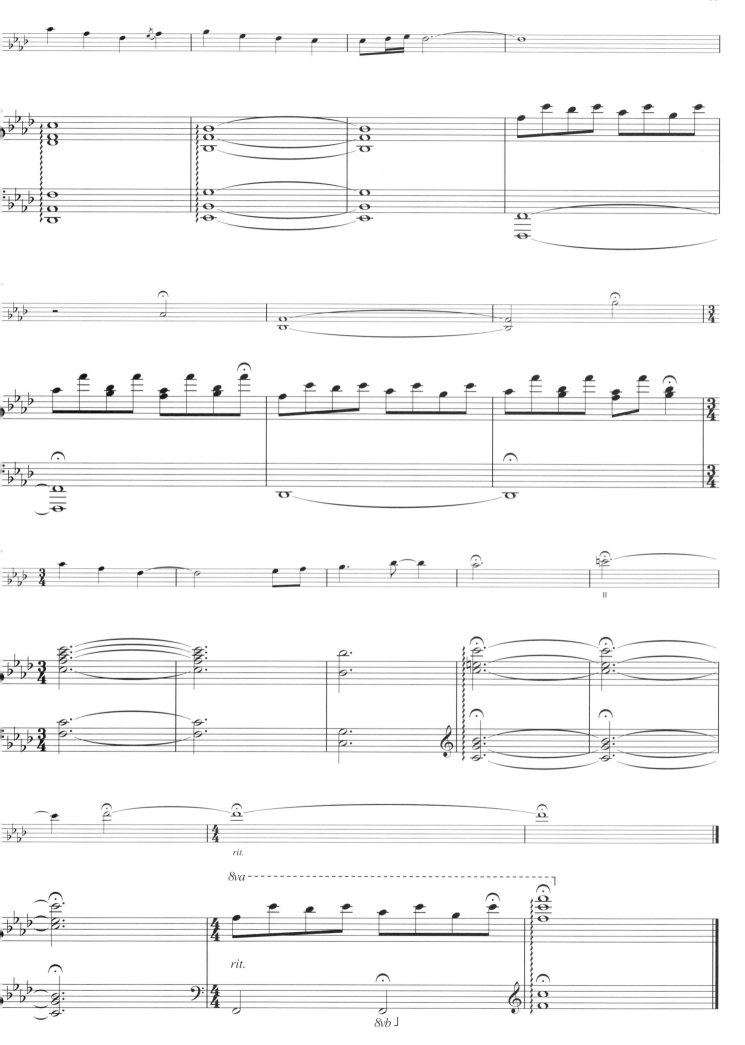

As performed by The Piano Guys

GOOD KING WENCESLAS

Arranged by JON SCHM
AL VAN DER BEEK and STEVEN SHARP NELS

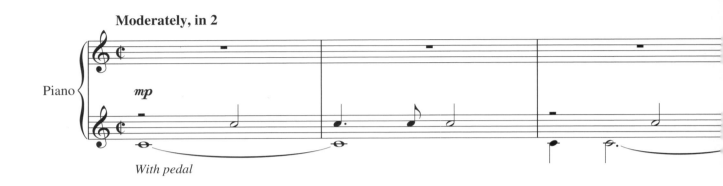

Repeat and Fade

Optional Ending

As performed by The Piano Guys

WHERE ARE YOU CHRISTMAS?

from DR. SEUSS' HOW THE GRINCH STOLE CHRISTMAS

Words and Music by WILL JENNINGS
JAMES HORNER and MARIAH CAREY
Arranged by JON SCHMIDT
AL VAN DER BEEK and STEVEN SHARP NELSON

Moderately, expressively

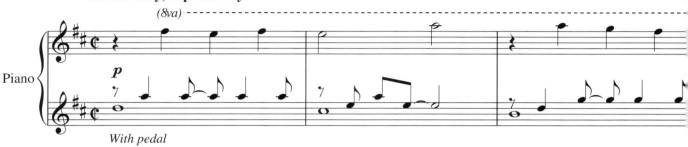

Moderately slow, expressively

Piano solo: play vocal melody 8va

I feel you, Christ - mas. I know I've

found you. You nev - er fade a -

love.

Fill your

heart with love.

As performed by The Piano Guys

LET IT SNOW!/WINTER WONDERLAND

LET IT SNOW!
Words by SAMMY CAHN
Music by JULE STYNE
Arranged by STEVEN SHARP NELSON
and AL VAN DER BEEK

WINTER WONDERLAND
Words by DICK SMITH
Music by FELIX BERNARD
Arranged by STEVEN SHARP NELSON
and AL VAN DER BEEK

*Multiple cellos arranged for piano

più legato

*Play 8vb if desired

As performed by The Piano Guys

STILL STILL STILL

By JON SCHMIDT

Slowly, very expressively

With pedal

Bring out melody

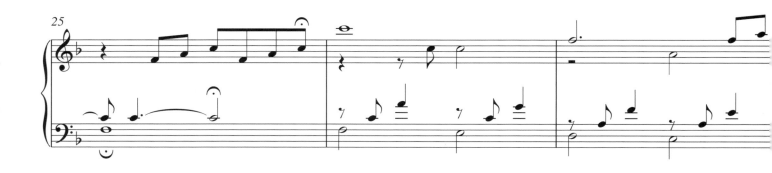

Bring out L.H. melody

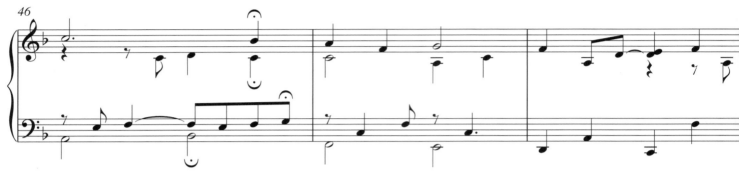

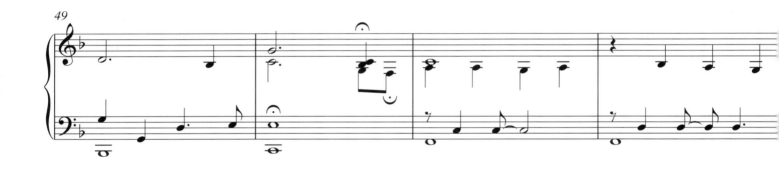

As performed by The Piano Guys

WE THREE KINGS

Arranged by STEVEN SHARP NELSON,
JON SCHMIDT and AL VAN DER BEEK

As performed by The Piano Guys

CHRISTMAS MORNING

By JON SCHMIDT

Moderately fast

Small hands delete notes in parentheses

As performed by The Piano Guys

WINTER WIND

By JON SCHMIDT
Cello arranged by STEVEN SHARP NELSON

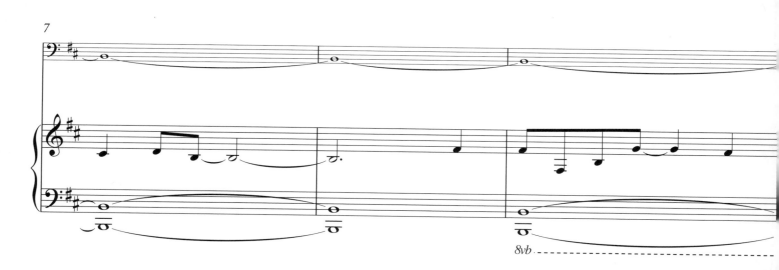

Bring out L.H. melody

simile

As performed by The Piano Guys

SILENT NIGHT

Arranged by JON SCHMID
AL VAN DER BEEK and STEVEN SHARP NELSO

Slowly, very freely

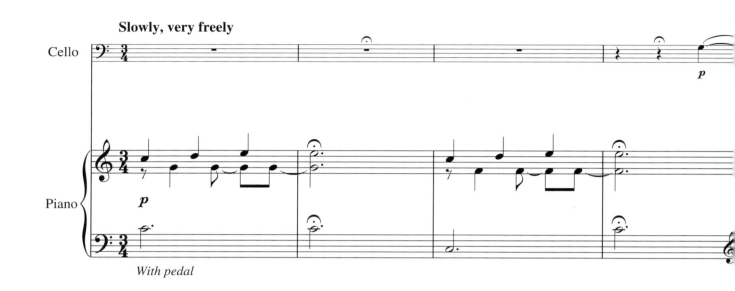

thy ho - ly face, with the

dawn of re - deem - ing grace.

Je - sus, Lord at thy birth.